OET SPEAKING FOR NURSES BOOK 1

By Virginia Allum

© OET Speaking for Nurses Book 1 by Virginia Allum

2017

All rights reserved

Contents

1. Introduction to the Speaking Sub-test

2. Building a Relationship with the Patient
   - Scenario: Child with Burns
   - Teenage Boy with Scurvy

3. Understanding the Patient's Point of View
   - Scenario: Dealing with Complaints

4. Conducting the Role Play using a clear structure
   - Scenario: Dog Bite

5. Asking for information and showing understanding
   - Scenario: Irritable Bowel Syndrome

6. Providing information and checking understanding
   - Scenario: Sleep Apnoea

Introduction to the Speaking Sub-test

A NOTE ABOUT THE UPGRADED OET SPEAKING SUB-TEST

After September, 2018, the OET format for the Listening and Reading Sub-tests will change slightly.

THERE WILL BE NO CHANGE TO THE FORMAT OF THE SPEAKING SUB-TEST, that is, two (2) role plays will be performed, each of 5 minutes duration.

There is a minor change to the assessment of the role plays, in that from September, 2018 the updated OET will also assess clinical communication skills. Clinical communication skills are the skills needed to communicate confidently in the workplace.

Examples of these skills include:
- **relationship building** (helping a patient to feel comfortable, when discussing concerns with you,

building a feeling of trust between the nurse and the patient)

- **understanding the patient's perspective** (showing empathy and understanding especially in situations where patients are anxious or worried, e.g. because they do not understand their treatment)

- **providing structure to the conversation** (being able to 'signpost' information, so patients are ready to listen to what is said)

- **establishing what a patient already knows** (working out, whether to build on existing knowledge or start from the beginning, when patients do not have any prior knowledge of their condition or its treatment)

- **gathering information from the patient** (showing a range of questioning skills, confirming information which is unclear and summarising)

The general principles of the role plays remain:
- the candidate (playing the role of a nurse) should always initiate and control the role play

- any medical information needed for the role play should be contained in the role play. If candidates are unsure of a medical term, they should make the best guess of what would be appropriate to say in the context of the role play. For example, if the role play is about a respiratory condition, phrases about breathing, tightness in the chest, coughing or sneezing would be appropriate, where phrases about indigestion or bowel movements would not.

1. What is the Occupational English Test (OET) like?

The Occupational English Test or OET is a medical English test for any of 12 health care professionals who want to register within their profession in an English-speaking country. The 12 professions include Nursing, Medicine, Pharmacy, Dentistry, Optometry, Occupational Therapy, Radiography, Dietetics, Podiatry, Physiotherapy, Veterinary Science and Speech Pathology.

Nursing is the most commonly represented profession, followed by Medicine. You may notice the absence of some healthcare professions, such as Social Work and Psychology. Candidates from these professions may choose to sit the test for a different profession.

The OET can be seen to be divided into two parts:
Reading and Listening: all professions do the same papers
Speaking and Writing: specific to each profession, e.g. nurses do the Speaking role plays for nurses.
The topics in the speaking test relate to scenarios which are often experienced by nurses, however, the language functions, that is the way you communicate are common to all professions.

So, to repeat the important part about the role plays. **They are a test of your ability to communicate**. They are not a test of your knowledge of the medical condition which is the subject of the role play.

This is the difference between the OET role plays and the sort of role plays you may have done through OSCAS or OSCES during your degree.

Objective Structured Clinical Examination (OSCE) also called Objective Structured Clinical Assessment (OSCA) tests your clinical (nursing) knowledge in a particular area as well as your ability to communicate with the patient.

The OET concentrates on your ability to communicate during a scenario without performing clinical tasks. During an OSCE, a nurse will be observed communicating with a patient while performing a range of nursing activities. The clinical setting is duplicated to make the scenario as authentic as possible. All forms of communication will be available for the nurse to demonstrate competence: verbal and non-verbal.

During the OET role play, the candidate will play the part of a nurse in a non-clinical environment. That is, you, as the nurse will sit opposite an interlocutor who plays the part of a patient or relative of a patient. You will not demonstrate clinical skills and will mainly communicate in a verbal way, by speaking. It is only possible to convey non-verbal communication using tone of voice, as the scenario is recorded as an audio tape, not a video recording.

The structure of the Role Play

The speaking test contains an initial warm-up conversation and two role plays.

The warm-up conversation

This is a brief (2 minute) chat where the interlocutor checks and confirms your details. Remember that if you use an 'English' name but your passport uses your birth name, you may have to explain this. Be ready to explain the reason for using different names, e.g. *'My English name is Jenny. It's easier than my Korean name, Sug Ja.'*

Even though the 2-minute chat is not given a mark it is a great opportunity to relax a bit and build a rapport with the interlocutor. Try to look as though you are enjoying yourself. Smile and maintain eye contact. If you appear confident and relaxed, it makes the job of the interlocutor a lot easy.

It also gives you an opportunity to check that you are happy with the volume of the audio recording. You may need to sit a little closer to the microphone or speak up.

Examples of Warm-up Conversations

The short warm-up conversation about you and your professional background.

This will be around 2 minutes long. You should try to have a few sentences planned for each possible question. Things which you might talk about:

1. *What do you know about life in Australia/UK/NZ?*

Asking what you know about famous landmarks e.g.

'What do you know about the wildlife in Australia?'

What do you know about the lifestyle in New Zealand?

Have you ever visited the UK before?

2. *What are your plans when you live overseas?*

This question could be about whether you plan to just work or perhaps travel as well. You could talk about study plans. You may plan to stay for a few years then return home.

3. *Why do you want to work overseas?*

This is where you explain whether you want to work overseas to experience a different culture, to learn new skills or because you feel you will have more opportunity.

4. *What is your current field of nursing?*

Explain the area of nursing you are involved in and the main activities you do, e.g. orthopaedic nursing in a trauma unit, medical unit specialising in burns treatment etc. You should learn the vocabulary which is appropriate to your type of nursing, e.g. 'fractures' (orthopaedic nursing).

5. What do you like about nursing? Try to think of three reasons you like the area you are working in, e.g. it's fast paced, the procedures are very interesting, it's very rewarding. If you don't like the area you work in, you could explain why, e.g. you don't feel that your skills are used in this area, you find the type of nursing very depressing etc.

6. Where will you work when you move overseas? Describe the area you are planning to go to even if it is still a plan, e.g. *'Are you looking at one of the big cities or a small town? Are you thinking of working in a remote area?'* Prepare three or four sentences which describe the place you are considering.

Your notes for the Warm Up Conversation

Building a Relationship with a Patient

- starting the role play appropriately
- being polite and respectful
- being an Active Listener
- showing empathy
- being non-judgmental

Starting the Role Play Appropriately

Look at your role play card and think about the person you are speaking to. Is the interlocutor playing the part of, e.g.

- an young adult patient
- an older patient
- an older patient with dementia
- the carer of a patient
- the parent of a young child

Now, think about how you will address the patient or carer. To establish a rapport with the patient or carer, you should try to be friendly, but respectful.

The role play card should guide you. For instance, the role play card says that you are speaking to a 22-year-old woman, called Judith. You would address her as 'Judith.' If the role play card says you are speaking to an elderly man, called Mr Fellows, you would address him as 'Mr Fellows'.

Remember that you don't have time to ask the question, *What would you like me to call you?* or *Do you mind, if I call you by your first name?*

Also, be aware that it is not appropriate to call a patient or carer *Madam, Mam* or *Sir*.

Think about how you will introduce yourself to the patient or carer. These days, nurses use their first name to introduce themselves, e.g. *Hello, I'm Sam* (not *Hello, I'm Mr Jeffries*).

Remember to add your designation, e.g.

Hello, I'm Sam, one of the nurses in Accident and Emergency.

or

Hello, I'm Sam, one of the RNs in Accident and Emergency.

Being an Active Listener

The term **Active Listening** refers to the ability to take an active part in the listening process and, more importantly, demonstrate an interest in what you are listening to. It is the opposite of **passive listening.** Examples of passive listening are listening to the radio or a podcast. While you are listening, you can't give any feedback to the person speaking.

On the other hand, when you listen to someone actively, you give feedback in the way of body language or sometimes 'listening noises'. When you listen actively, you are respectful of the other person and are able to pick up important information.

Unfortunately, there are many barriers to effective listening. These are often called **communication blocks**. These blocks stop you getting your message across and can also stop you from receiving messages in return.

Sometimes people are not aware that they are setting up blocks and wonder why they are not able to communicate easily with patients and colleagues.

There can be a variety of barriers to communicating effectively. These barriers fall into 4 groups:

1. Physical barriers:

These are caused by anything which affects the body. For example,

- **Speech difficulties** like slurred speech, a stammer, aphasia or dysphasia (after stroke or a brain injury)
- **Hearing impairment**: including times when hearing aids are not used.
- **Sight impairment**: be aware that the sight impaired also pick up on non-verbal communication even though it may be in a different way.
- **Confusion,** e.g. in dementia: it may make it difficult for a confused person to follow the conversation and respond appropriately.
- **Pain**, especially severe pain which makes it difficult to concentrate.
- **Fatigue or altered consciousness,** including tiredness caused by medication.

2. Environmental Barriers

- **Space or distance between people**

Patients who are lying in bed with a nurse standing 'over' a person may not feel an equal participant in the conversation. Nurses who stand at the end of the bed when talking with a patient make the conversation seem like a quick exchange.

Noise

loud noises or loud music can affect patients' ability to concentrate. If a conversation is important or sensitive, it is a good idea to minimise noise or music by going to a different location or asking for the music to be turned down.

- **Physical**

the arrangement of furniture in certain configurations can make a conversation seem formal or serious. For example, chairs in a straight line are less welcoming than chairs in a circle or semi-circle. A desk between patient and nurse also creates a barrier.

- **Environment**

This can be anything from room temperature to the number of people in the room. Rooms which are large but contain a small number of people can seem confronting and make people feel that there is too much attention on them.

3. Social and Cultural Barriers

- **Low level of health literacy**

patients who have little knowledge of medical procedures or medical conditions may struggle to follow the conversation and may tune out.

- **Heavy accent or pronunciation problems**

An accent which is hard to follow can create barriers to understanding. Regional English accents can be difficult for non-native speakers as well as native-speakers.

- **Inappropriate use of jargon or medical terminology**

it is important to judge the ability of patients to understand medical terminology. Some terms have become common in general use, e.g. hypertension whilst others are not common and therefore not easily understood, e.g. tachycardia. Nurses should also be aware of the number of terms used between colleagues (jargon) which may not be understood by patients.

- **Intercultural factors**

this includes different expectations of the role of the nurse and also the effect of different types of non-verbal communication between cultures. Gender may be an issue in cases where nurses are not used to caring for patients of the opposite sex.

4. Psychological Barriers include:

- **Anxiety, fear or stress**

These factors affect the ability to listen clearly or listen to more than one or two instructions.

- **Anger or aggression**

Patients or their relatives who are angry about their treatment may not be willing to listen to what a nurse is saying.

- **Conflicting verbal and non-verbal messages**

non-verbal communication such as pitch of voice or lack of eye contact which does not match the words used cause confusion for the listener.

Being Polite and respectful

It is important to speak to patients in a respectful way, but at the same time ensuring that you show warmth and care for them. Sometimes patients behave in a manner which is not their usual way of behaving. This may be, because they are in pain or concerned about their welfare or the welfare of their relative.

Think of some scenarios, where patients may behave in a highly emotional way. Perhaps they are:
- in acute pain, e.g. admission to Accident and Emergency with back pain after an injury
- very worried about a diagnosis, e.g. waiting for the result of a breast cancer biopsy

- concerned about their child, e.g. child admitted with paracetamol poisoning
- sick of waiting for surgery, e.g. have experienced their surgery being cancelled a few times

Showing Empathy
Empathising versus Sympathy
There is a clear difference between **sympathy** and **empathy**. Sympathy is a close feeling of sorrow felt for the other person. Nurses who feel sympathetic about a patient's situation may identify with a situation, having experienced something similar themselves. Unfortunately, they may become overwhelmed by their feelings and not be able to maintain professional boundaries.

On the other hand, empathy is the ability to imagine the sadness or distress a patient may be feeling. It is sometimes said that you put yourself 'in the shoes' of the other person, to try to imagine the sorrow they feel. Empathetic responses indicate that you are trying to feel and understand something of what the other person is experiencing whilst retaining personal boundaries.

Listening Empathetically

Firstly, observe what the patient is experiencing and try to understand how a patient may feel when they experience these things. Then, try to identify what the patient may need.

Examples of role plays where empathetic responses may be used:
- a mother of a young child with burns
- a young mother with a baby who may be jaundiced
- a grandmother who is anxious about her grandson's epilepsy
- a mother who is concerned about whether to vaccinate her child or not
- a mother with a child who is being admitted to hospital for the first time

Firstly, imagine how the child's mother may be feeling. The mother may:

- be very upset
- feel guilty because she left her daughter unsupervised in the kitchen
- be worried about possible scarring
- want information and advice about First Aid and care at home

The nurse may have to:

- calm her: ask her to slow down / repeat information (Note: Never say 'Calm down' – it has the opposite effect)
- reassure the mother that she did the right thing in bringing the child to hospital promptly
- explain what might happen next /about treatment
- give advice about follow up care

Scenario: Child with Burns

Vocabulary

accidental

burn

superficial burn

partial thickness burn

full thickness burn

scald

scar /scarring

Medical Terms: Types of Burns

You may find burns referred to as:

first degree burn	superficial burn
second degree burn	partial thickness burn deep dermal burn
third degree burn	full thickness

Communication Focus: Language Used in the Role Play

1. Empathising and Reassuring

Notice that the nurse says, 'Try not to worry', not 'Don't worry'. This is an important difference.

I can see that you are very upset. Try not to worry too much, you did the right thing by bringing your daughter to hospital so promptly.

I appreciate how hard this is, but you should try not to be too concerned; you couldn't have done more.

I know it's very difficult, but you did the right thing so try not to worry.

2. Helping the patient to explain what happened

This is called **facilitating.**

Can you tell me what happened?

Can you tell me how your daughter burned herself?

Can you tell me how your daughter got burned?

How did your daughter get the burns?

3. Asking a person to slow down

In this role play, the nurse asks the mother to slow down, so she can understand better.

Could you slow down a bit. I can't follow what you're saying.

Could you speak a bit more slowly? I'm having trouble following what you're saying.

4. Clarifying information

Asking the mother to repeat information which the nurse didn't understand.

Can you repeat that last bit – I didn't quite catch it.

Can you tell me what you said again, I didn't understand it.

5. Talking about possible consequences

She might have some scarring.

She might have to use some cream for a few weeks to treat the burns.

It's possible that she may have some scarring but there are good treatments now.

There's a chance that she may have a bit of scarring.

6. Explaining a procedure using steps

You'll need to bathe her arm in mild soapy water.

Just apply a thin layer of cream to the burns then put on a non-adhesive dressing.

Make sure you put on a bandage from her wrist to her upper arm to keep the dressing on.

7. Giving Follow up information

I have a patient information leaflet here with some information for you.

You can find the Emergency number at the bottom of the leaflet.

Watch the video on YouTube at https://www.youtube.com/watch?v=SyZKTtDW_E4
Identify the following communication skills in the dialogue.

initiates the conversation appropriately

1. is respectful
2. shows empathy and reassures
3. is non-judgmental and picks up cues
4. asks open-ended questions
5. clarifies information which is not understood
6. explains procedures in an organised way
7. signposts a change in the topic
8. pauses between steps of an explanation
9. offers further information

Watch the video again and follow the transcript. The transcript is at the end of the book. Put a number (as above) next to the communication skills you hear.

Being Non-judgmental

Some role plays include opportunities for you to demonstrate **non-judgmental language. Judgmental language** is the type of language where a person is critical or blames another person for something. In healthcare, an example of this might be:

You really should lose weight, because you're much too fat.

This is the sort of language which is to be avoided in the role plays. Whilst a person who is overweight should lose weight to be healthy, it may be more helpful to say something like:

It might be a good idea to try to lose a bit of weight, to benefit your health.

Notice that the sentence used the phrase *'It might be'*, rather than *'You should'*. Also, the **softener** *'a bit of weight'* was used.

Some of the role plays which might have opportunities to demonstrate non-judgmental language include those about:

- lifestyle changes, e.g. quit smoking, do some exercise
- dietary changes, e.g. eat less, eat more, reduce fat/fibre/sugar

Sometimes during the role play your 'patient' will try to make it a bit more difficult for you. For instance, the patient may be resistant to making changes which will benefit their health.

Scenario: Teenage Boy with Scurvy

Vocabulary

bleeding gums

a bruise

bruising

deficiency

kiwi fruit

mango

pill

scurvy

source

Vitamin C

Do you know what scurvy is?

Look at the vocabulary list above and try to guess a bit about the condition. Put relevant terms under the correct headings. Some terms may be used more than once.

Cause	Symptoms	Treatment

Look at a role play between a school nurse and a teenage boy who is being encouraged to change his diet. He explains that he doesn't eat much fruit at all.

Watch the video on YouTube at
https://www.youtube.com/watch?v=qz55GRYa068
Try to identify the following communication skills:

1. initiates the conversation appropriately
2. is respectful
3. reassures
4. is non-judgmental and picks up cues
5. asks open-ended questions
6. clarifies information which is not understood
7. explains procedures in an organized way
8. signposts a change in the topic
9. pauses between steps of an explanation
10. offers further information

Watch the video again and follow the transcript. The transcript is at the end of the book. Put a number (as above) next to the communication skills you hear.

Understanding the Patient's Point of View

- avoiding communication barriers
- picking up verbal and non-verbal cues
- identifying patient concerns
- managing difficult conversations
- poor communication versus good communication

Communication Barriers

There are many barriers to effective listening or communication blocks. These blocks stop you getting your message across. Sometimes people are not aware that they are setting up blocks and wonder why they are not able to communicate easily with their patients.

There can be a variety of barriers to communicating effectively. These barriers fall into 4 groups:

1. Physical barriers:

These are caused by anything which affects the body. For example,

- **Speech difficulties** like slurred speech, a stammer, aphasia or dysphasia (after stroke or a brain injury)
- **Hearing impairment** – including times when hearing aids are not used.
- **Sight impairment** – be aware that the sight impaired also pick up on non-verbal communication even though it may be in a different way.
- **Confusion** e.g. in dementia – it may make it difficult for a confused person to follow the conversation and respond appropriately.
- **Pain** – especially severe pain which makes it difficult to concentrate.
- **Fatigue or altered consciousness** - including tiredness caused by medication.

2. Environmental Barriers:

- **Space or distance between people.** Patients who are lying in bed with a nurse standing 'over' a person may not feel an equal participant in the conversation. Nurses who stand at the end of the bed when talking with a patient make the conversation seem like a quick exchange.
- **Noise** – loud noises or loud music can affect patients' ability to concentrate. If a conversation is important or sensitive, it is a good idea to minimise noise or music by going to a different location or asking for the music to be turned down.
- **Physical** – the arrangement of furniture in certain configurations can make a conversation seem formal or serious. For example, chairs in a straight line are less welcoming than chairs in a circle or semi-circle. A desk between patient and nurse also creates a barrier.
- **Environment** – this can be anything from room temperature to the number of people in the room. Rooms which are large but contain a small number of

people can seem confronting and make people feel that there is too much attention on them.

3. Social and Cultural Barriers:

- **Low level of health literacy** – patients who have little knowledge of medical procedures or medical conditions may struggle to follow the conversation and may tune out.
- **Heavy accent** – An accent which is hard to follow can create barriers to understanding. Regional English accents can be difficult for non-native speakers as well as native-speakers.
- **Inappropriate use of jargon or medical terminology** – it is important to judge the ability of patients to understand medical terminology. Some terms have become common in general use e.g. hypertension whilst others are not common and therefore not easily understood e.g. tachycardia. Nurses should also be aware of the number of terms used

between colleagues (jargon) which may not be understood by patients.

- **Intercultural factors** - this includes different expectations of the role of the nurse and also the effect of different types of non-verbal communication between cultures. Gender may also be an issue in cases where nurses do not care for patients of the opposite sex in a particular culture or religion.

4. Psychological Barriers include:

- **Anxiety, fear or stress** – These factors affect the ability to listen clearly or listen to more than one or two instructions.
- **Anger or aggression** - Patients or their relatives who are angry about their treatment may not be willing to listen to what a nurse is saying.
- **Conflicting verbal and non-verbal messages** – non-verbal communication such as pitch of voice or lack of eye contact which does not match the words used cause confusion for the listener.

Examples of Poor Communication

1. Being Defensive

This may happen when patients or their relatives complain about what they consider to be poor nursing care. The nurse may reply: *'It's not my fault. I do what I can when I have time but I'm very busy.'*

2. Changing the subject inappropriately

The nurse may feel uncomfortable about what the patient is saying and not know how to reply. E.g. *'Oh…ah, well, let's get this dressing done now, shall we?'* Instead of discussing the patient's concerns about dying, the nurse changes the subject and talks about the patient's dressing.

3. Offering false reassurances

by suggesting that: *'Everything will be fine'* or *'I'm sure that the lump probably won't be cancerous'*, the nurse is saying what s/he thinks the patient wants to know. It may be done to reassure, however, it can affect the trust between the nurse and the patient and affect future communication.

4. Offering advice or giving an opinion
Of course there are times when you are supposed to offer advice or an opinion, however, there are other times when merely listening is appropriate. By 'jumping in' and giving advice before the patient has finished talking, the patient may feel that the nurse is not interested in the conversation.

5. Ignoring non-verbal cues
Non-verbal cues are often culture-based so may be difficult to pick up. There are differences even within English-speaking countries, e.g. the UK, USA and Australia. It's a good idea to be aware of non-verbal cues which you may be expected to use. Some of these are maintaining eye contact, nodding your head to indicate agreement and using 'listening words' like 'Mm' or 'Uh huh'.

6. Inappropriate means of communication

The selection of a medium of communication may be inappropriate for the message. All oral communication – face-to-face, by telephone, by phone or on television- may be misheard. If the speaker cannot be seen, there is no opportunity of picking up non-verbal cues. Sometimes it is important to follow up verbal communication with written communication. A common example is the need for a written consent before an operation. A verbal consent is not appropriate nor is it legal.

7. Using language which is too complex:

Medical terminology can be difficult for lay people. The trend for using 'plain English' means that nurses are expected to explain procedures using the everyday language understood by patients.

Checklist for Sending a Clear Message

1. **Use clear language.**

Avoid jargon. Clearly state what it is you want the other person to understand.

2. **Check that your message has been received** with no misunderstanding.

If you have any doubts, get the receiver to repeat to you the content of your message.

3. **Repeat if necessary**, without impatience if you think the receiver has not understood your message.

4. **Ensure content is appropriate** to the comprehension level of the receiver.

Simplify if necessary, but avoid child-like dialogues.

Non-verbal Communication

Non-verbal behaviours *add meaning* to speech. This is called *meta-communication* or a 'message *about* a message'. Non-verbal communication helps to work out what a person's message is about.

Non-verbal communication is *congruent* if it matches what is being said. For example,
No, I'm not too busy to help you. (said while smiling and looking at the patient) – congruent because the nurse means to say that s/he is happy to help and is not too busy to help.

No, I'm not too busy to help you. (said with a sigh and while looking at his/her watch) – incongruent because the non-verbal communication indicates that the nurse thinks s/he is too busy to help and is annoyed at being asked.

Kinesics

Kinesics is the study of body movement. Facial expressions, gestures and eye movements are the most common categories.

- **Facial Expressions** – movements of the face which communicate emotions.
- **Body movements and gestures** – the way you lean forward or lean back shows how much you want to be near another person.
- **Hand gestures** can communicate anxiety or impatience.

Eye contact

The amount of eye contact you feel comfortable with may relate to your cultural background where eye contact may be considered rude or inappropriate. In another culture, lack of eye contact may equally be considered inappropriate or even dishonest. Maintaining eye contact for the correct amount of time differs from staring which makes people uncomfortable.

Proxemics of use of Personal Space

The distance we stand from another person is also dictated by culture. People from some cultures feel comfortable standing quite close to another person where the same distance would be construed as causing discomfort in another culture. Generally, people from an Anglo-Saxon background like to have an arm's length between them where many Europeans are quite comfortable standing much closer to each other. This distance is sometimes called a person's 'personal space'.

Therapeutic Touch

Touching another person when speaking to them especially in situations where the other person is upset or distressed is called 'therapeutic touch'. Therapeutic touch may involve a touch on the forearm or on the shoulder.

There are times when therapeutic touch can be effective, however, it is very difficult to achieve. It is important to be aware of the feelings of the other person towards being touched by a stranger. Young nurses may find it difficult to know if an elderly patient would welcome a touch on the arm or may find it condescending.

Managing Difficult conversations

People in distress can find it difficult to listen to what you are saying and may not be able to respond appropriately. One example of a difficult conversation is when dealing with aggressive patients or relatives. Role plays which concern patients or relatives who are annoyed or angry can be challenging. There are some useful tools which can help you in dealing with these sorts of situations.

One of the main causes of frustration for patients and their relatives is delay in treatment, for example an operation which is postponed. It is important to try to imagine the emotions patients and relatives go through when this happens. Remember that the patient is probably anxious about the surgery and its outcome. They will have been fasting for several hours to prepare for the operation, so they are probably hungry and thirsty.

Added to these emotions is the very powerful feeling of loss of control over their environment. Some unlucky patients have their operation postponed not just once but twice or three times. Sometimes an angry response results from the hope that it may influence the surgeon to go ahead with the operation anyway.

There are several actions which you should avoid when you are dealing with patients or relatives who are distressed or behaving in an aggressive manner. It is important not to try to restrain the person at all. This includes touching the person on the arm or shoulder and using restraints. Restraints can only be used after a medical assessment is made and a medical order is completed.

Try not to react to bad language – overlook language even if it is personal if possible. If the person is delusional, reorient them to reality. It is, however, important not to be defensive or blame someone else for the perceived problem. At all times attempt to calm the environment by asking the person to speak a little quieter so you can understand better.

A common cause of distress and anger in patients' relatives is delay in treatment. Look at the sample role play card for a nurse and imagine how you would react. Then, read the transcript of a dialogue between a nurse and the relatives of a patient whose operation has been delayed.

Scenario: Dealing with Complaints

Before you start, review these terms:

to clarify   to make something clear, after you realise the listener does not understand you

to persuade   to convince someone to do something

Read the nurse's role play card. What communication skills do you think you will demonstrate in this role play?

Sample role play:

Setting: Hospital Ward

Nurse: You are talking to your patient's daughter who is angry about her father's care. Your patient's daughter is threatening to take her father out of hospital.

Task:

1. Find out about the patient's daughter's concerns
2. Explain the delay in her father's surgery
3. Empathise about the situation and offer solution
4. Persuade the daughter not to take her father home.

Watch the video at https://www.youtube.com/watch?v=RMh-zNvF_kk

Identify the following communication skills:

- explaining a delay without blaming other staff members
- empathising about a difficult situation
- overlooking insulting language
- persuading someone to remain in hospital
- helping the patient or relative to explain the difficulty
- clarifying that you have understood

Watch the video again and identify the language the nurse uses for the following:

1. How does the nurse empathise and finds out why the patient's daughter is upset?

2. What does the nurse NOT do, when the patient's daughter says, 'You people are useless'?

3. How does the nurse confirm that she has understood what the problem is?

4. Instead of blaming the Recovery staff, how does the nurse manage the situation?

5. The nurse has to persuade the patient's daughter to leave her father in hospital, so he can have his operation. She does this in steps. What were they?

Review: Good versus Poor Communication

Write the correct number next to the following examples of <u>poor communication.</u> Number 1 is done for you.

    Being reluctant to discuss sensitive or embarrassing issues

    Not Giving Verbal Feedback to show understanding

    Having Poor Anger Management

1   Not explaining clearly

    Interrupting Frequently

    Using clichés

    Showing a Lack of Empathy

    Assuming you understand without listening properly

    Not giving Non-Verbal Feedback to indicate interest

    Not clarifying information

    Being flippant

Poor	Solutions: Good Communication

Communication	
1.	1. Structure the message in steps, so that it is clear what you are explaining. 2. Limit the explanation to 3 pieces of information. 3. Use signposting, e.g. *Firstly…Then…Finally…*
2.	If you need to interrupt, try to use an interruption as a means of confirming that you understand. E.g. *Can I just interrupt for a moment? I want to be sure that I understand what you are saying.*
3.	Use active listening skills to make sure that you really hear what the patient says.
4.	1. If you are unsure of anything,

	always clarify what you think the patient is saying, even if you are embarrassed to admit you don't understand. 2. Do this by repeating what you think the patient said. E.g. *So, what you are saying is….., right?*
5.	1.Start by being honest about your difficulties with the topic, e.g. *I know it is difficult to discuss these things, but it may be helpful so we can make some arrangements for you.*' (talking about moving to a hospice for end of life care) 2. Understand that the patient may also be embarrassed
6.	Never use clichés (phrases which are overused) to avoid talking about

	sensitive issues. For instance, *'Don't worry, time heals all wounds.'* (to a relative after the death of a patient).
7.	Don't downplay what patients say or they may feel that they are being 'spoken down to' and are not an equal partner in the conversation. For example, *Come on now, it's not that bad. It's only a scratch!*
8.	1. It is important to empathise with an angry patient before you continue the conversation. E.g. *I can see that you are very upset at the moment. Can you explain a bit more what the problem is?* 2. If the patient or their relative speaks louder and louder, ask them to lower their voices before you

	continue. E.g. *Before we go on, could you speak a bit quieter, so I can understand what you are saying.*
9.	1. Empathy is the ability to **imagine** what the patient is feeling rather than say that you **know** how they are feeling. Avoid saying *I know how you feel. I had the same thing, so I know all about it.* Use Empathetic responses: *You must be feeling very worried about your daughter.* *I imagine that you must be concerned about the surgery.*
10	1. Use Feedback to ensure that patient and nurse understand what is being said. e.g. *I see. So, you are saying that you*

	have been in pain for the past day. Is that right?
11	Feedback may also be non-verbal. For example, nodding your head to show agreement, narrowing your eye brows to show you are unsure of what is being said.

Conducting the Role Play using a clear structure
- providing structure to the role plays
- keeping control of the role play
- planning for the time limit of the role play
- signposting to explain procedures in an organised way

Providing Structure to the Role Plays

During the Speaking sub-test, you will perform two role plays of 5 minutes each. The topics of both role plays will be different. The second role play will follow immediately after the interlocutor informs you that your time is up for the first role play.

Each role play card guides you how to conduct the role play through a list of tasks. The role play needs to follow a definite structure, so that you can cover all points in the allotted time. In fact, most conversations, especially those in a clinical setting, tend to follow a similar pattern.

After you have looked at the tasks on your role play, you should have an idea of the language the interlocutor will be expecting to hear from you. In other words, what is the purpose of the role play? Is it:

- to give information or explain treatment
- to persuade the patient to do something or not to do something
- to empathise with the patient
- to give advice

You should be able to draw on some expressions which you have practised beforehand. But starting the role play is sometimes difficult. In authentic conversations, you will have been taught to ask open questions to encourage the patient to talk. The OET asks you to do this while doing most of the talking yourself.

Think about how a conversation might flow:

1. You introduce yourself and explain your title or role.
2. You ask some questions to find out what has happened.
3. You explain what is going to happen now.
4. You give advice about lifestyle changes, new medications or discharge activities.
5. You 'round off' your conversation

Some conversations take different turns, e.g. if the person you are talking to doesn't agree with something you are saying or is not convinced about what you are saying. In this case, you may have to add some other strategies like persuading, empathising or reassuring. This makes the role play sound a bit more authentic.

The role play card should contain any medical knowledge that you may need. If you are unsure of a medical term, you may ask the interlocutor before the role play starts.

There are two paths the conversation may take. The first possibility is that <u>you</u> will start the conversation. The second possibility is that the 'patient' will start it off. Remember that you won't have the benefit of seeing the patient's role card so it will be guess work in the beginning.

Planning the role play

As you plan your role play, think about some important features of the role play:

1. You need to build a relationship with your patient in a short space of time.
2. The role play should flow in a logical way from one task to another.
3. You need to show that you are an **Active Listener** and can pick up on the cues the patient may be giving you about their concerns.

4. You should be confident in using the most appropriate questioning form to gather information about the health issue.

5. You should be confident in providing information or advice to the patient and making sure it is understood.

Some of the things you should keep in mind, when doing the role play:
1. ways to explain medical terms using everyday language to your patient. Always keep in mind the level of knowledge you think the 'patient' has. If you don't use terms the patient understands, there may be a serious misunderstanding.

When you learn new terms, it's a good idea to make a glossary of the terms and their equivalent everyday terms. This includes terms which might be quite formal, e.g. *reduce*. Some people may understand better, if you use the phrasal verb *cut down*. Start with these:

reduce	cut down
eliminate	cut out
remove	take out
sutures	stitches
IV	drip

2. focusing on communication skills. What assessors are looking for is whether you can start a conversation with a patient, keep it going, manage the conversation if the patient tries to be difficult and then close the conversation. Don't forget that the interlocutor is not an assessor, but a type of actor, playing the part of a patient.

What can I do if I don't know anything about the topic?

As I said before, you will usually be given any information you need on the role play card. However, sometimes you may have to make a guess at the meaning of an unfamiliar term.

An example of this is a role play between a school nurse and a teenage boy who has scurvy. If you didn't know what scurvy is, you could guess that it has something to do with problems with the diet as later in the role play you are asked to advise the student about some diet changes he should make.

But, what if you can't guess at all what the condition or disease is? Or, you don't know what a medication does. You can do a bit of inventing. After all, we want to hear you explaining the condition or the medication.

You can use expressions like these:

1. *'X is a condition that affects your skin.'*
2. *'Condition Y causes some problems with your digestion.'*
3. *'Medication B is a tablet that lowers your blood pressure.'*
4. *'You need to be careful when you take the medication. You should always take the tablets before a meal.'*

As you can see, you can always make very general statements about medical conditions. If you are talking about a medication, you can talk about how to take it, warn about side effects and advise how long to take the medication. Remember that it doesn't have to be accurate information; it's the way you give advice that's important.

So, in summary try not to worry too much about your medical knowledge. It is more important to concentrate on communicating well.

Go over the expressions you know for the most common communication examples.

Practise the pronunciation of some sample dialogues. Be aware of any pronunciation areas which you find difficult and practise them. For example, you have difficulties pronouncing *deterioration*. Break the word into syllables and say it slowly. Start saying the word a little quicker, then put the word in a phrase, e.g. *deterioration in her condition.*

If you can, try out a sample role play on a friend. Or listen to the patient speaking before writing and saying your own answer.

Write your own role play and practise it. Or, use dialogues in preparation materials.

Time your role play so you have an idea of how a 5 minute role play should flow. Finally, try out some alternative phrases.

Keeping Control of the Role Play

During the speaking test, you should make sure that you are in control of the conversation. You are expected to start things off and to maintain the flow of the conversation. This is what is referred to as sequencing a conversation in a logical manner.

In the real world, of course, you would be trying to encourage the patient to speak as much as possible. You would make sure that your conversations were patient-centred not nurse-centred. You would ask open questions to get the person to talk more.

During the OET speaking test, you need to be doing the talking most of the time. You still need to ask open questions, but you should also ensure that you display your communication skills to your best advantage.

Keep in mind that the interlocutor and the assessors want to see how well you can communicate. The assessors will listen to the tape of your conversation afterwards and mark your performance. Correct grammar is quite important but sounding natural and developing a rapport with your 'patient' is just as important.

The sort of communication skills you need to show are:
1. introducing yourself and opening the conversation
2. asking open questions to encourage the patient to speak
3. using closed questions when necessary
4. taking turns in the conversation/interrupting politely
5. Signposting a change in the topic of a conversation
6. Organising pieces of information in an explanation
7. summarising what you have said or what the 'patient' says
8. encouraging the 'patient' to change or try something
9. clarifying information which is not understood

10. explaining terms in a way that the listener can understand

11. using varying tone of voice

12. indicating that you are an active listener

13. asking for co-operation

14. closing or 'rounding off' the conversation

Challenging Factors in a Role Play

You won't know what direction the 'patient' is going to take the conversation but you can assume that the 'patient' will try to be a bit difficult at some stage of the role play. This is often done to see, how well you can keep control of the conversation.

Some of the things a 'patient' may do:

1. The 'patient' keeps talking, e.g. the patient may be upset about something that has happened. You need to politely 'jump in' and move the conversation back on track, e.g.

'Can I just interrupt you for a minute? I'd like to make

sure that I understand what you are saying.'

'Can I just stop you now? I want to check that I understand correctly.'

Then, you might summarise what the 'patient' says to confirm that you understand, e.g.

'So, what you said was that you were walking on the street, then you fell over a rock and injured yourself.'

Try to confirm understanding using steps.

2. The 'patient' won't say much.

The patient may just answer your questions with one or two words. You are going to have to encourage the patient to open up, by asking open questions, e.g.

'Can you tell me a bit more about what happened?'

'Can you explain again what happened?'

If the 'patient' still answers with one word or two, you can summarise what was said, e.g.

'I see. So, you are saying that........'

'OK. So, you told me that....'

You could also empathise with the 'patient' if this is relevant, e.g.

'I imagine that must have been very difficult for you.'

' That must have been very upsetting.'

3. The 'patient' tries to get you off track.

You may be trying to explain something when the 'patient' tries to move the conversation in another direction. You will have to politely redirect the 'patient' where you want the conversation to go. E.g.

'I can talk about that in a little while. Can we just get back to what we were talking about first?'

'Can I stop you there, please? I can see that you are upset about that. I will explain about that in a minute.'

4. The 'patient' is un-cooperative and won't follow your advice.

In this case, you need to negotiate with your 'patient'. Some possible situations:

- a teenager has scurvy but doesn't like fruit and vegetables
- an elderly gentleman refuses to have new tablets because they are the wrong colour
- a young mother insists on taking her baby home even though the baby is jaundiced
- a patient refuses to return to hospital for a dressing change, because he doesn't want to take time off work

You can use expressions such as:

'Would you be willing to try eating more oranges.'
'Would you be willing to wait until the blood results come back?'
'Could you just wait for a few minutes while I check your results?'

Planning for the Time Limit of the Role Play

You have five minutes for each role play. You could plan it out like this:

< 1 min   Introduce yourself and say what your title is. Here are some examples:

1. *Hello, I'm Virginia. I'm the Registered Nurse looking after you today.'* (the role play is set in a hospital ward.)
2. *'Hello, thanks for coming in today. I'm Virginia, one of the Registered Nurses at this clinic.'*
(the role play is set at a Community Medical Centre.)
3. *'Hello, I'm Virginia, the School Nurse. Thanks for coming to see me.'* (the role play is set in a school.)

3-4 mins - Go through the tasks on your role play card. Notice that there may be two issues per role play. Both issues often relate to each other.

There are usually four tasks on each card. One may be *'Find out more about …'* – this is the beginning of the conversation where you hear what the problem is. Then, perhaps an *'Explain about x disease and its treatment'* – you will talk about the kind of disease it is, how it may affect the patient and how it is treated.

What if I don't know anything about the disease on the role play card?

Remember that the role play is a language test. If you don't know what the disease is, describe any disease in general terms. E.g.

'I'll just explain a bit about the condition. It can be quite a serious condition if you don't look after yourself. You'll have some tests first to check your blood and possibly also a scan. The doctor will talk to you about that a bit later. I will explain everything about the tablets you'll be taking after you have the tests.' – as you can see, this could be any illness!

You can explain medication in general terms as well – *'The tablets you are going to take make you feel a little sick if you take them on an empty stomach. It's a good idea to take them with a meal or a dry biscuit.'*

Practise the sort of language you would use to describe a disease or condition before you do the test. It's a good idea to learn the phrases you will use, e.g. 'take the whole course of antibiotics'.

1 min - Closing the conversation.
If you have time, summarise the conversation. You can say:
'OK. We've talked about x, y, z.'
'Just to go over what we talked about...'

Then, you can suggest that the 'patient' may like to read a leaflet about the problem:
'I have a leaflet here which will explain a bit more about burns/scurvy/IBS etc. There's a number on the back which you can call for more information.'
'I'll give you this leaflet to read. Call me if you have

any more questions after you've read it.'

Or, you can ask if the 'patient' has any questions he or she would like to ask.
'Do you have any questions you'd like to ask?'
'Is there anything else you'd like to ask?'

Signposting

Signposting refers to the way that we point towards what is coming up in a conversation. It is, as if we are holding up a sign to the listener explaining that we are about to move to another topic or the next step in an explanation.

An example of the way signposting can be used is in explaining a procedure to a patient.

In order to explain a procedure during a role play there are several factors to think about.

- Use everyday language rather than medical terminology where possible. Assume that your patient doesn't have or has limited knowledge of medical procedures.

- Try to structure the explanation in steps of no more than three parts. This way you can use **signposting terms** like *Firstly, secondly, lastly.*

You can prepare explanations and practise them before the test. Think about the sort of things you are likely to need to explain to a patient and the vocab you might need.

Examples of procedures which might be explained easily using signposting:
- doing a dressing for a burn
- looking after a dressing including removal of stitches
- taking pain relief after an operation
- having a blood test
- having a tetanus injection

As well as signposting, clarifying language should be included to ensure that you understand what the patient has said. This also shows that you are listening carefully to the patient.

Scenario: Admission to A&E after a Dog Bite

Vocabulary

injection (jab)

sutures   (stitches)

tetanus

Scenario: Dog bite

The dog bite role play contains several explanations.

You need to:

- explain about the dressing to the bite
- explain the lack of sutures
- explain the need for a tetanus jab

Watch the dialogue at

https://www.youtube.com/watch?v=1xNGKxWVr6s

What does the nurse talk about with the patient?

1.
2.
3.

This role play differs from other role plays in that the nurse has to explain why sutures (stitches) are **not needed**. Watch the video again and identify how the nurse explains this.

Explaining what is NOT going to be done.

1. _____
2. _____
3. _____

Look at the nurse's role play card. Notice how the tasks give you a structure for your role play.

Topic 1: The dog bite
- appearance of the wound
- treatment in hospital (clean wound / no stitches/ dry dressing over wound)
- care at home (do dressing every 2 days/ keep dressing clean and dry)

Topic 2: Tetanus jab

- ask when last had one
- advise one now
- persuade to have tetanus jab

Watch the video again and identify the two parts of the role play.

Setting: Accident and Emergency

Nurse: You are attending to a woman who has sustained a dog bite on her leg. She was brought to hospital by her friend. The wound will not need to be sutured (stitched), but she will need a tetanus shot.

Task:

1. Find out about the wound (the dog bite)
2. Explain what treatment will be given in hospital
3. Give advice about wound care at home
4. Explain need for a tetanus jab
5. Persuade the patient about importance of tetanus jab.

During the role play, the nurse explains that she is going to give the patient some advice about care of the wound at home.
Watch the video and put the steps of her advice in the correct order.

don't get dressing wet, when showering

nurse will give patient dressings to take home

do dressing every two days

cover dressing with plastic bag, when showering

Persuading
During the role play, the patient is not happy about the idea of having a tetanus injection. The patient suggests reasons, why he would prefer not to have an injection. Complete what the nurse says in the role play.

Patient: Oh look.. I really don't want an injection. I hate them. And, it's only a dog bite. Aren't they quite clean?
Nurse: No, unfortunately, dog bites _____

_____.

And you need to protect _____

_____.

Patient: Are you sure it's necessary? Can't I wait and see, if I develop any symptoms. Then I'll have the shot.

Nurse: I can understand that you don't want an injection, if it's not necessary, but _____

_____.

It really is very important that you protect yourself against tetanus. It can _____

_____.

Asking for Information and Showing Understanding

- **using different question types: open and closed**
- **explaining procedures**
- **clarifying information which is not clear**
- **summarising information to ensure understanding**

Using Different Question Types

Open Questions

Open questions are those which encourage a person to speak more about a topic, rather than give a 'Yes' or 'No' answer.

You can ask open questions in several ways:

Can you tell me about ...?

Can you tell me how long...?'

Can you tell me what...?'

Grammar Point: Can you tell me...?

Be careful with *'Can you tell me about...'* as it may be followed by a noun or a verb (with some changes).

'Can you tell me about …..noun / gerund?'

'Can you tell me about what/how/when/why/where….verb….?'

Example 1:

'Can you tell me about <u>the pain</u>?

Can you tell me <u>when you get</u> the pain?'

Example 2:

'Can you tell me about <u>your leg ulcer</u>?

Can you tell me <u>where the ulcer is?</u>'

The verb in a *'Can you tell me where/what/who ….?'* is in reverse.

1. *Where **did** you **take** your son?*

    *Can you tell me where you **took** your son?*

2. *What medication **do you take**?*

    *Can you tell me what medication **you take**?*

3. *What **is** your name?*

    *Can you tell me what your name **is?***

Closed Questions:

Closed questions are used to get a quick answer or perhaps a fact. For instance, if you want to know a person's date of birth, you would ask a closed question (*What is your date of birth?*) An open question would not be appropriate.

Examples of Open and Closed questions

Example 1. bedwetting role play

Closed: '*How often does he wet the bed?*' – you'd expect the patient to say, '*Every night*' or '*He wets the bed all the time*'.

Closed: '*Can you tell me how often he wets the bed?*' – similar to the previous question

Open: '*Can you tell me about his bedwetting?*' – Notice that I had to use a noun form (gerund)

Example 2:

'What caused your daughter's injury?' - **closed**

'Can you tell me what caused your daughter's injury?' - **closed**

'Can you tell me about your daughter's injury?' – **open** question

A variation is *'Can you tell me a bit more about your daughter's injury?'*

Review: Types of questions

- Open questions: often use the modal **'can'**

Make sure you know the correct structure: Can + verb. The verb 'explain' may also be used.

- Avoid a common error :

Can you explain <u>to me</u> NOT ~~explain me~~

Can you tell me a bit about + noun?   Can you tell me a bit about the pain?

Can you explain about +noun? Can you explain about the nausea you experience when you eat?

Can you explain to me how often you get muscle aches?

- Closed questions: often use :

Do you?

Are you?

Have you?

'Wh' questions

Do you + verb?   Do you have any serious medical problems?

Don't you + verb? Don't you realise how dangerous it is to mix your medications?

Are you + verb?   Are you allergic to anything?

Aren't you + verb? Aren't you doing any exercise at all?

Have you got any + noun? Have you got any questions?

Haven't you got any + noun? Haven't you got any health problems at all?

When do you + verb?   When do you notice the pain?

Grammar Point: *Can you tell me about + verb*

If you want to use a verb with the 'Can you tell me about' expression, you need to add a 'wh' question word onto it.

Example 1:

What happened to your daughter?

*Can you tell me about **what** happened to your daughter?*

Example 2:

*How often **does** your son **have** this problem?*

*Can you tell me a bit more about **how often** your son has this problem?*

Example 3:

*Why **are you** concerned?*

*Can you tell me a bit more about **why** you are concerned?*

Notice that the order of words changes in these questions:

Grammar Point: Can you tell me about + prepositions

Be careful with the placement of prepositions in a question. If you are starting the conversation and are unsure of the reason for the patient's visit, you may ask:

- *Can you tell me what you are concerned **about**?*
- *Can you tell me what you are worried **about**?*
- *Can you tell me what you have difficulty **with**?*
- *Can you tell me what you have problems **with**?*

Notice that the preposition goes at the end of the question.

The role play cards usually contain around 4 tasks for you to cover. You should aim to cover all tasks in the 5 minute speaking time.

The first task is the cue for the start of the role play. The first task gives you a starting point for your conversation.

A common first task is a 'Find out about..' task. Some examples are:

1. Ask about.... or Find out about....

1. Scurvy: Ask Jake about his diet and lifestyle.
2. Bedwetting: Find out the out the frequency of bedwetting and if there are any other concerns.
3. Young child with epilepsy: Find out as much as you can about the boy's condition.
4. Immunisation: Find out exactly what the patient's concerns are.
5. Child with burns: Find out as much as you can about the accident and subsequent treatment of the burns.

6. Parkinson's Disease: Find out what the patient is having difficulty with.

7. Head injury: Find out as much as you can about the details of the patient's accident and any symptoms.

8. Appendectomy: Find out as much as you can about the details of the patient's accident and any symptoms.

Other 'first tasks' are:

Give the patient information about... or Explain...
- Baby with jaundice: Give the patient information and advice on the condition.
- Explain the positive aspects of total hip surgery
- Explain why you are monitoring a patient who has just had a stroke

Try to persuade....
- Resident in Nursing Home: Try to persuade the resident to take his/her medication

Discuss patient concerns

- Child with meningitis: Discuss the parents' worries

The Nurse Starts the Role Play

If you are starting the conversation, it's important to introduce yourself and explain your position in the ward or community centre. You'll find out the information about this on the role play card. Look at the 'Setting' for some direction e.g. *'Hello, Mrs Smith. My name's Virginia. I'm a Registered Nurse on this ward.'* The setting may be a ward, the Accident and Emergency Department, a school or a workplace health centre.

If the patient starts the conversation, it may sound a little strange to introduce yourself as it may be accepted that this has already happened. As the patient starts talking, use Active Listening techniques to indicate that

you are paying attention and being respectful to the patient. You'll remember that Active Listening may be:
- nodding your head
- saying *'Uh huh'*, *'Oh right'* and *'Mm'*
- smiling

Then, you can look at the 'find out about' question, that is, why the patient is talking to you. During this stage, it is important that you not only listen to the patient's words, but also pick up non-verbal cues. The patient may sound hesitant or find it difficult to put their concerns into words .

Confirming Understanding of Information

In some role plays, the nurse asks for information about symptoms, like pain or nausea. In some cases, patients have difficulties explaining how they feel, e.g. what their level of pain is. This may mean that the nurse has to clarify understanding of the information.

Sometimes, if the information is about a sensitive topic, patients may be embarrassed to talk initially. Clarifying the information may be necessary in these cases too.

Scenario: Irritable Bowel Syndrome

Vocabulary

bloating

constipation

cramps

diarrhoea

digestive

flare-up

gas-producing

intestinal

laxative

stools

wind

watch the video on YouTube at
https://www.youtube.com/watch?v=0xb8f3LS2mQ

Identify the statements and questions you hear.

1. Asking about the frequency of symptoms

How often have you had these symptoms?

How many times a year do you have the symptoms?

How frequent are the bouts of IBS?

How long do the symptoms last?

2. Asking about the type of pain

What does it feel like when you have the bouts of IBS?

Can you tell me what the pain's like?

What type of pain do you get?

What is the pain like?

3. Giving advice to a patient with IBS

You need to take the tablets when you have any pain?

You should use the tablets to control the symptoms.

It's a good idea to increase the amount of water that you drink as well.

It would be a good idea to make some dietary changes.

You might like to think about eliminating high fibre

foods from your diet.

It's advisable to avoid gas-producing foods like cabbage.

Try to avoid stressful situations if you can.

But, you will need to cut out high fibre foods.

4. Confirming information

So, what you're saying is that you have episodes of diarrhoea and abdominal cramps around three times a year?

What I understand is that you have these bouts of abdominal bloating every month. Is that right?

Can I just check what you are saying? You mentioned that you have episodes of diarrhoea and constipation every few week. Is that correct?

So, you have a type of colicky pain and flatulence. When you say that you have to keep going to the toilet, do you mean that you have diarrhea or constipation? Or both?

Setting: Gastroenterology Clinic

Nurse: You are the nurse who works at the Gastroenterology Clinic. You are speaking to a 25-year-old who has just been diagnosed with Irritable Bowel Syndrome and is not sure about the condition. She also needs advice about treatment and management. You need to gather information about the symptoms she experiences to be able to give her advice on management of the condition.

Task:

1. Find out about the symptoms she experiences
2. Find out about any triggers she may have noticed
3. Explain what IBS is in simple
4. Explain management including non-pharma management

Watch the video again and answer the questions.

1. The nurse starts the conversation by ...

A   asking why the patient has come to see her

B   confirming that the patient has IBS

C   asking how the patient manages her condition

2. The nurse ...

A   clarifies the type of pain the patient experiences

B   does not understand the meaning of 'colicky'

C   gives advice about the patient's pain

3. The nurse clarifies information about...

A   how long the diarrhea lasts

B   the frequency of the episodes of diarrhoea

C   how many times the patient goes to the toilet

4. The nurse explains that stress...

A   is the cause of IBS

B   is a consequence of IBS

C   may contribute to IBS

5. The nurse advises the patient to…

A   cut out high fibre foods

B   increase fibre in her diet

C   cut out all fibre in the diet

6. The IBS patient information leaflet contains…

A   supporting information about the condition

B   contact details for the IBS Support Group

C   a phone number to call, if patients are concerned

Providing information

- finding out what the patient already knows
- preparing to give information
- making suggestions
- giving advice
- giving strong advice
- offering further information

Finding out what the Patient already knows

Before providing information to patients, it's a good idea to find out what the patient already knows about their health issue. This is called **Health Literacy.**

Patients who are well informed about their condition may not need a general explanation about the condition. They may only want specific information. For example, the patient has had arthritis for many years and understands the effect of the condition. However, the patient has recently put on a lot of weight and is finding that her joints are becoming more painful and she is unable to mobilise easily.

In this case, the nurse would not waste time explaining what arthritis is and how it affects your joints. The focus of the role play would be the reasons for the weight gain and questions about the effect of the weight gain on the patient's ability to manage daily activities.

Care must be taken in role plays, where the patient appears to have a lot of knowledge about their condition, but it has not come from a reliable source. They may say:
I was reading about my condition in a magazine and it said that I should do xyz.
I was talking to my neighbour. He had the same condition as I have and he takes xyz.

This may be said to get you 'off track' or as a way of refusing to follow advice.

Preparing to give information

The first step in preparing to give information is to think about the type of information you are about to provide to the patient, e.g.

- explaining a procedure
- explaining a treatment the doctor has prescribed
- explaining follow up care
- making a suggestion
- giving advice
- giving strong advice

The next step is to break down the information into **chunks.** This makes it easier for the patient to understand. During the role play, it gives the nurse an opportunity to demonstrate a number of communication skills, e.g.

1. signposting the next step in the explanation

The first thing that I'm going to talk about is the effect of weight loss on your joints.

Then, I'll tell you about some mobility aids which may help you.

2. clarifying information

You may have to repeat information in a different way, so that the patient understands what you are saying, e.g.
What I mean by that is ...
Another way to explain that is...

You may have to clarify information, if you use a medical term which a patient doesn't understand, e.g.
The term 'apnoea' means 'without breathing' or 'not taking any breaths.

3. summarising

At the end of an explanation, you can summarise the main points to make sure you have got an important message across to the patient, e.g.
In summary, I spoke about x and y and z.
Reviewing what I said, I talked about x and y and z

Finally, breaking information into chunks is a useful strategy during the role play, as it helps you keep the explanation within a short time. Limiting your explanation to three steps means that you will not run over time. Remember that your explanation will not be a complete explanation. Keep in mind that you are being assessed on your language skills, not your understanding of a clinical scenario.

Look at the following examples:

- **explaining care of a dressing at home**
    1. keep it clean and dry
    2. change dressing every 2 days
    3. return to GP to have stitches out in a week
- **explaining falls prevention in the home**
    1. keep the floor free of clutter
    2. keep a light on in the bathroom at night
    3. wear shoes with non-slip soles

Try to avoid giving too much information, as you don't have time during a short role play (5 minutes). Some candidates find this difficult, because they tend to think about the amount of information they would provide in a real scenario.

Giving Advice and Making Suggestions

Think about the times when you may need to give advice.

* before a patient is discharged home (advice about dressings, removal of sutures)
* before taking a new medication
* using a piece of equipment (CPAP machine, nebuliser)
* making lifestyle changes (weight loss, quit smoking, increasing exercise)

What about making suggestions? A suggestion may follow a piece of advice. You may be helping the patient to see ways that s/he can follow your advice, e.g.

* starting to exercise more by taking a short walk at first with a friend.
* setting a realistic goal of the number of cigarettes to be smoked each day in decreasing numbers
* starting a diet diary to note down all the food which is eaten each day to pin point problem areas in the diet.

Giving advice about sensitive topics

There are some topics which are quite difficult to advise on, e.g. reducing alcohol consumption which is excessive, the need for incontinence aids, unsightly scars. As with persuading, it is important to first acknowledge that it may be embarrassing for the patient to discuss the problem. *I understand that it might be difficult for you to talk about this but it is very important that I give you some information.*

These functions range from the gentle to the essential.

1. Making a suggestion

which patients can choose to accept or not, but the choice will not affect their health

Have you thought about + ing?

What about + ing?

Why don't you try + ing?

2. Giving advice

informing patients in order to improve their health

It would be a good idea to + verb

It's not a good idea to + verb.

It would be helpful to + verb

It's not helpful to + verb.

You should try to + verb

Examples: Giving advice

It's advisable to wait for the test results.

It's wise to give the baby water while he is having phototherapy.

It's important for you to stay in hospital overnight.

It's not a good idea to go home before you speak to the doctor.

It would be a good idea for you to stay here.

It's not necessary to stay any longer.

It's essential that the baby stay in hospital during the treatment.

It's not advisable for you to take the baby home yet.

Persuading: giving advice or making suggestions when the patient is reluctant

What can you do if the patient refuses your advice or is reluctant to follow your suggestions? Always remembering that patients have the right to accept or refuse advice, try to think of ways that you can persuade the patient to accept at least part of your advice.

Would you be willing to try to cut down smoking a little? (the patient has said s/he doesn't want to give up smoking at the moment)

3. Giving strong advice

giving information which is essential to follow to avoid serious health problems

You must + verb

You mustn't + verb.

It is essential that you + verb.

It's essential that you don't + verb.

Do not + verb.

Review: Expressing an opinion or giving advice

Positive sentences	Negative sentences
It is (It's) + adjective + infinitive *It's wise to drink water in the evening rather than coffee.*	**It is not (isn't) + adjective + infinitive.** *It's not essential to do all the exercises at once.*
It is (It's) + adjective + for pronoun + infinitive *It's important for you to take it easy.*	**It is not (isn't) + adjective + for pronoun + infinitive** *It's not advisable for you to drive after the operation.*
It is (It's) adjective that + subjunctive *It's essential that you take all the medication in the packet.*	**It is not (isn't) + adjective that + subjunctive** *It's not necessary that he use the crutches.*

Scenario: Sleep Apnoea

Vocabulary

daytime sleepiness

fatigue

insomnia

snoring

Look at the nurse role play card below. Remember that you will only see your role play card (nurse) so you will have to guess what the patient will say to you. Look at the nurse's card and think about the topics you will cover:
1.
2.

Nurse Role Play Card: Sleep Apnoea

Setting: Medical Centre

Nurse: You are a GP Practice Nurse who has been asked to talk to a 65-year-old patient about sleep apnoea. He is going to attend a Sleep Clinic for assessment but doesn't understand why. He is obese but not keen on losing weight. He also needs to use a CPAP machine (type of oxygen mask which keeps the airways open) but does not know much about it.

Task:

1. Find out the history of the problem.
2. Explain why sleep apnoea can be a serious condition
3. Explain the function of CPAP
4. Give advice on lifestyle changes
5. Persuade patient to follow lifestyle change advice

Watch the video at
https://www.youtube.com/watch?v=9ckOJ6Tg02g
Match the language functions with examples from the video.

1. Finding out the history of the problem
2. Signposting what you are going to talk about
3. Explaining a health condition using everyday terms
4. Reinforcing the importance of information
5. Empathising
6. Explaining medical terms

7. Using non-judgmental language
8. Encouraging a lifestyle change
9. Giving an alternative point of view

Number _____

Sleep apnoea is caused by the throat closing for short times during sleep. This closes the upper airway, so breathing stops. After a short time, the brain realises that breathing has stopped and triggers breathing again. This can sound like snoring.

Number _____

Can you tell me what sort of health problems you've been having?

Number _____

I'll explain a bit about sleep apnoea and why it can be a serious problem, if you don't manage the condition.

Firstly, we advise you to avoid drinking alcohol or take medication which may make you sleepy.

Number _____ *I can see it's a bit of a shock for you and a lot to take in,*

I appreciate that it seems overwhelming

Number _____

The important thing to remember about the condition is that it is not simply a form of insomnia or a type of snoring. If it is not managed properly, it can be serious condition.

I appreciate that it seems overwhelming, but it really is very important to take as much pressure off your throat area.

As I said before, sleep apnoea can be a serious condition.

Number _____

How would you feel about not drinking alcohol or limiting your intake to a small amount?

Number _____

It's called a CPAP mask. CPAP means continuous positive airways pressure.

Number _____

How would you feel about not drinking alcohol or limiting your intake to a small amount?

Would you be willing to look through this leaflet on nutrition and weight loss?

Number _____

Yes, that's certainly true, however, excess weight, particularly in the neck area also plays a big part in your ability to breathe well, when you are lying down.

Giving further advice: Patient Information Leaflets

Patient information leaflets are found in all hospital areas. They are produced to help patients and their relatives understand medical conditions and medical treatment. The leaflets may also contain phone numbers of support groups which patients or their relatives may find helpful.

You can also use patient information leaflets at the end of the role play. When you are rounding off the conversation you can offer the patient a leaflet and suggest that they read about the things you have been discussing. They can call the number on the leaflet if they have any questions.

Transcripts:

Chapter 2: Building a Relationship

Dialogue: Child with Burns

Nurse: Hello. It's Mrs Smith, isn't it? I believe your daughter got burnt last night. Can you tell me how it happened?

Patient's mother: I was cooking dinner last night. I was busy and I got distracted. I shouldn't have done it. I know I should have taken more care. The phone rang and I went out of the kitchen to answer it.

Nurse: That's OK. Take it slowly. I want to make sure I understand correctly. So you were cooking dinner last night and what happened then?

Patient's mother: I was cooking rice and my daughter wanted to see what I was doing. She wanted to see how much rice I was cooking. That's when she tipped the hot water on herself. And when she burned herself.

Nurse: I see. That must have been very frightening for you. And for your daughter.

Patient's mother: It was awful. It happened so fast too.

Nurse: Yes, it can happen very fast. Can you tell me what you did first, you know, to do something about the burns?

Patient's mother: All I could think of was to take my daughter's shirt off and soak it in cold water. I put the wet shirt over the burns on her arm. Did I do the right thing? I just did what I thought was right.

Nurse: Yes, you did the right thing. People used to put butter on burns but it's the worst thing you can do. You made the right choice.

Patient's mother: But I feel so guilty. Look at her arms. She'll have terrible scars.

Nurse: I know it looks awful now but it will look a lot better when the burns start to heal. Try not to feel guilty. Children at this age are very inquisitive. They just want to look at everything, but they don't realise the dangers. Scalds on the arms especially the hands and fingers are very common. And scalds most often happen in the kitchen.

Patient's mother: But I shouldn't have answered the phone! If only I had stayed in the kitchen. I don't know. I feel so bad.

Nurse: I can see that you feel bad about the accident, but I think it's important to focus on what we are going to do now to treat the burns. OK?

Patient's mother: Oh yes. OK. What happens now? What are you going to do? She's in a lot of pain.

Nurse: The first thing I'll do is to give her something for the pain. Then, when the pain is under control I'm going to wash her arm very gently and put on some special cream to help stop infection. The last thing is to make sure she is drinking enough. Can you help with that?

Patient's mother: Yes, sure. I'll give her sips of water whenever I can.

Nurse: That's great.

Patient's mother: Look, I'm really worried about the scarring. I want my daughter to see a specialist now, before it gets worse.

Nurse: I know your daughter's skin looks bad now because her skin is very red. Your daughter will need to have dressings to the burns for quite some time, but it will look better, once the skin starts to heal.

Patient's mother: Yes, but I'm still worried about the scarring. Isn't there anything that can be done about it?

Nurse: After the burn has healed, your daughter will be seen by a burns specialist to look at any scarring. I know it's difficult, but the skin has to heal first. There are some very good treatments these days so please try not to worry too much.

Patient's mother: OK, but it's difficult to take it all in!

Nurse: I know it is difficult to remember everything, so you might find this leaflet helpful.

Read through the leaflet and ask us, if you have any questions. There is also a contact number at the bottom of the leaflet.

Chapter 2: Building a Relationship

Dialogue: Teenage Boy with Scurvy

Nurse: Hi Jake, My name's Irene. I'm the school nurse. You wanted to see me today?

Patient: Yeah. Look, I'm a bit worried about these bruises. And I've got all these red spots too.

Nurse: I see. Where's the bruising, Jake?

Patient: On my legs, all over them. And I've got these red spots everywhere.

Nurse: Right, yes I see. Have you been to your GP about the bruises?

Patient: Yeah, I went to the doctor a month ago. He said something about scurvy but that's only not having enough vitamin C, isn't it? That won't cause these bruises.

Nurse: I can see you might be a bit confused, but it's right. Scurvy is a condition that you get if you are not getting enough Vitamin C in your diet. Vitamin C is important for making sure that your body can use iron properly. It also helps to strengthen the tissues of your blood vessels. If you don't have enough your gums will start bleeding and you'll bruise very easily.

Patient: Oh really? I didn't know that. The doctor just said I should eat better. Anyway, the drinks I drink have vitamins in them.

Nurse: Some drinks have added vitamin C but it's actually better to eat fresh fruit and vegetables. Do you eat a lot of fresh fruit and vegetables?

Patient: Um. No. I don't like fruit much. Mum doesn't like it either, so she doesn't buy much.

Nurse: The thing is, Jake, that a vitamin C deficiency can be quite serious if it goes on too long. If you don't take in enough vitamin C your gums start bleeding and your teeth become loose. They can even fall out, in the very worst cases.

Patient: I didn't know all that. I didn't think vitamins were so important.

Nurse: Yes, they are. Some vitamins can be stored in the body, but vitamin C can't be stored for more than a short time. That's why I asked, whether you like fruit and vegetables. Vitamin C has to be taken in everyday because it isn't stored. The best source is in fruit and vegetables. Some have more vitamin C than others. Oranges and lemons and other fruit like kiwifruit, mangoes and strawberries are high in Vitamin C. The best vegetables are cabbage, spinach and broccoli.

Patient: So, I can't just take a vitamin C pill?

Nurse: Well, you could take a pill, but it doesn't help you long-term. Do you like any of the fruit that I mentioned?

Patient: Um, I don't mind mangoes and kiwifruit are OK. So, you're telling me that the bruises are because I don't have enough vitamin C?

Nurse: That's right. The bruises are a sign that you need more vitamin C, that you are not taking in enough vitamin C every day.

Patient: If I start getting more vitamin C, how long before the bruises go?

Nurse: If you get enough vitamin C each day, the bruises will go quite quickly. As a teenage boy, you need around

75mg of vitamin C each day. Just remember, that it can't be stored at all.

Patient: Yeah. I understand. I'll get onto it and get Mum to help as well.

Nurse: That's great. I'll give you this leaflet to take home with you. It has a lot of information about the best fruit and vegetables to eat to increase your Vitamin C intake.

Chapter 3: Understanding the Patient's Point of View

Dialogue: Dealing with Complaints

Patient's daughter: Well, finally! Can you tell me why my father is still in his bed when he should be having his operation right now? I'm really sick of this. You people are useless. How difficult is it to take an old man to his operation on time?

Nurse: I can see that you're very upset. It would help if I understood a bit more about the problem. Can you tell me a bit more about what's going on?

Patient's daughter: Well, thank goodness. Finally someone is asking! I've been here with Dad for hours just sitting and waiting. He was supposed to go for his operation at 10 o'clock. He hasn't had a thing to eat or drink since yesterday. Someone just said he couldn't go for the operation yet but didn't tell us why. Now we don't have any idea when or if he'll have his operation. If it goes on too much longer, I'm going to take him home. It can't be worse than being here.

Nurse: I can see why you must be very frustrated by all

this. If I've understood you correctly, you are frustrated about the delay in the operation and feel that you haven't been kept informed of the reasons for the delay and when your father is likely to have his operation? Is that right?

Patient's daughter: Yes. That's it. No-one has bothered to tell my father anything. They've just left him here starving and waiting for an operation that might never happen. It's not right doing that to an old man.

Nurse: It does seem very harsh when you haven't had a drink all night and are probably very hungry. I can help you out with that after we've had our chat, Mr Bigley. You can rinse your mouth out with a small amount of water, as long as you don't swallow any.

Patient: That's sounds wonderful.

Patient's daughter: Well that's all very well and good but what about the rest of the problems?

Nurse: I know that the time for your operation was supposed to be 10 o'clock. I've just checked with Theatres to find out the reason for the delay.

Apparently the patient who was first on the list, before your father, had a few difficulties after his operation.
Patient's daughter: That's not Dad's fault. Why should he have to wait?
Patient: Come on, Sally. These things happen.
Patient's daughter: No, Dad. These things don't just happen. They should know about these things and fix them.
Nurse: I can understand that you might feel that way. However, the staff in Recovery think that the previous patient should be all right soon which means that your father will be able to go for his operation.
Patient's daughter: Sounds like a cover-up. Dad, I think you should come home with me. I don't believe them at all.
Patient: Oh...I. I don't know, Sally.
Nurse: I know that it is hard when you have to wait so long but it is very important that you have your operation.
Patient's daughter: Well, I'm not so sure. If it was so

important, you'd have made sure he had the operation on time.

Nurse: I agree that treatment schedules don't always go to plan but it really is very important that your father stays in hospital. Would you be willing to wait a bit longer before you make the decision to take your father home or not?

Patient's daughter: I don't know. Dad shouldn't wait around for ever.

Nurse: I understand what you are saying. If I keep you up to date with what's happening, would you be willing to wait a bit longer?

Patient's daughter: I guess so. As long as we know what's going on.

Nurse: Yes. I'll make sure that I tell you how long your father will be waiting.

Patient: Thank you, nurse. I would appreciate that.

Chapter 4: Providing Structure

Scenario: Dog Bite

Nurse: Hello. My name is Mikaela. I'm one of the nurses in A &E. I believe that you've injured your leg. Can you tell me what happened?

Patient: I was walking to my friend's house when a dog rushed up and bit my leg. I was just about to open the gate to her house when the dog ran up. No warning at all!

Nurse: Right, I see. What does the bite look like?

Patient: It's sort of a gash on my lower leg. It's really deep. I'm afraid it's still bleeding and it's a bit of a mess.

Nurse: That's OK, I'll look at it in a minute. I'll just explain what I'll do now. First, I'll clean the wound with a lot of saline. Fortunately, the wound won't need any stitches. After I clean it, I'll put on a clean dressing.

Patient: OK, I see. But, it's a bit of a mess. Why won't I have any stitches?

Nurse: These days it's more common not to stitch dog

bites, especially if they are not big wounds. It's better to let the wound heal by themselves.

Patient: All right. I see. Is there anything else I have to do? Like at home?

Nurse: There are a couple of things you should do, when you go home. You need to do the dressing every two days. I'll give you some dressings to take home. Try not to get the dressing wet, when you have a shower. One way to keep the dressing dry is to cover it with a plastic bag, before you get in the shower.

Patient: OK. I can manage all that.

Nurse: Can you tell me when you had your last tetanus jab?

Patient: Oh! It must have been around 12 years ago.

Nurse: I see. You'll have to have a tetanus jab now.

Patient: Oh look.. I really don't want an injection. I hate them. And, it's only a dog bite. Aren't they quite clean?

Nurse: No, unfortunately, dog bites are actually very dirty. And you need to protect yourself against tetanus.

Patient: Are you sure it's necessary? Can't I wait and see, if I develop any symptoms. Then I'll have the shot.

Nurse: I can understand that you don't want an injection, if it's not necessary, but it really isn't advisable not to have a tetanus shot ,after a dog bite. It really is very important that you protect yourself against tetanus. It can be a serious disease.

Patient: All right, I suppose I should have the injection. I'll try to be brave, if it's so important.

Chapter 5: Asking for Information
Video: IBS

Nurse: Hello Jenny. Thanks for coming in to see me today. I believe you have just been diagnosed with IBS and need some information about how to manage the condition?

Patient: Yes, that's right. I had a test and now they are saying that it's IBS. I don't really know much about it.

Nurse: I see. Yes, it is a lot to take in at once. I'll explain about the condition in a minute, but I'd like to ask you a few questions about your symptoms first.

Patient: Oh OK.

Nurse: Can you tell me a bit about what's been happening with your bowels?

Patient: Well, uhm... I get awful abdominal cramps and pain. Uhm...and it's actually really embarrassing because I keep passing wind and I keep going to the toilet as well.

Nurse: It must have been very difficult for you. Can you tell me what the pain's like?

Patient: It's like a colicky pain in my stomach. A very

sharp pain.

Nurse: So you have a type of colicky pain and flatulence. When you say that you have to keep going to the toilet, do you mean that you have diarrhea or constipation? Or both?

Patient: What do you mean? I thought you have to have either diarrhoea or constipation.

Nurse: Not necessarily. There are a few different types of IBS. Some people just have constipation and some people have diarrhoea. Other people have both which is very unpleasant.

Patient: Oh, right. No, I just have diarrhoea but, as I said before, it's not all the time.

Nurse: I see. How long have you had these symptoms?

Patient: I've had the problem for around three months. Ah, yes, it started around three months ago.

Nurse: Can you think of anything which might have triggered the first attack? I mean, was there anything different happening in your life at the time?

Patient: Well, I started a new job around then. It was

very stressful especially at first. I have a lot of responsibility and I work long hours too.

Nurse: So, what you are saying is that the symptoms seemed to coincide with your new job?

Patient: Ah, yes. I suppose they did. Could it have something to do with getting IBS?

Nurse: Yes, it could be part of the reasons why you started having the episodes of bowel problems. When you feel tense and you can't relax, it can affect your bowels.

Patient: Oh, I'm afraid that I don't know anything about IBS. I'm very confused about it at the moment.

Nurse: It can be a lot to take in at once. I'll explain it to you now. IBS is a digestive condition which causes uncomfortable bowel symptoms. Some people have loose, mushy stools when they have a bowel movement. Alternatively, they might have hard stools and strain when they go to the toilet.

Patient: Do they know what causes it?

Nurse: No. The exact cause isn't known, unlike other

bowel conditions. In IBS, the structure of the intestines is quite normal but the intestines appear to be over sensitive at some times. That's what produces the bloating and intestinal spasms.

Patient: I see. Yes, I get bloating a lot. What about diet? Could there be something wrong with my diet?

Nurse: There are certain foods which make the condition worse. Can you tell me what kind of foods you tend to eat?

Patient: I always thought that I had a good diet. I try to eat a lot of vegetables and I like whole grain bread. I thought that was the best thing to do, but now I don't know what I should eat.

Nurse: A small amount of fibre in your diet is important to keep your bowels moving properly. But, you will need to cut out high fibre foods. It's a good idea to increase the amount of water that you drink as well.

Patient: OK. Is the fibre in my diet giving me the bloating?

Nurse: No, the bloating tends to be from gas-producing

foods like cabbage, for example. I'll give you a patient information leaflet on the foods which you should avoid to make it easier for you. Then you can try to avoid foods which cause you problems.

Patient: I see. I was told that my intestines were normal after the colonoscopy, so it was a bit confusing. I still don't understand it.

Nurse: It seems that the problem is that the intestines in IBS are overly sensitive and this seems to result in either constipation or diarrhoea.

Patient: Oh, I see. It's the sensitivity of the bowels that is the problem. What can I do about it?

Nurse: There are a few things you can do. I've already mentioned your diet and avoiding high fibre and gas-producing foods. The doctor will prescribe medication which will help with flareups of diarrhea and abdominal cramps It's also a good idea to think about some ways that you can reduce the stress in your life. Some people like yoga and meditation to reduce stress. Have you ever tried either of these?

Patient: No, but I'll give them a try. Anything to stop those awful cramps!

Nurse: That's great. I'll give you a leaflet about IBS now. There is a phone number on the leaflet for the IBS Support group. You may find that helpful too.

Patient: Right, thanks. That might be very useful.

Chapter 6: Providing information

Video: Sleep Apnoea

Nurse: Hello, Mr Gregson. I'm Grace, the Respiratory Nurse at the GP Practice. Thanks for coming in today to talk about your sleep apnoea with me.

Patient: Hello, Grace. I'm very confused about the condition. I'm not at all sure what I have to do now.

Nurse: That's OK, Mr Gregson. I'll explain about sleep apnoea and the treatment you'll follow. I'll also talk with you about some lifestyle changes which may help you as well.

Patient: OK, that would be very helpful.

Nurse: Before I start, can you tell me what sort of health problems you've been having?

Patient: I had a car accident 6 months ago and injured my nose. Since then I've been snoring all night, according to my wife. All I know is that I wake up exhausted every morning. I've had some tests which say that I have sleep apnoea.

Nurse: That's right. I'll explain a bit about sleep apnoea and why it can be a serious problem, if you don't manage the condition.

Patient: I thought it was the snoring that was the problem.

Nurse: No, sleep apnoea is different from snoring. Sleep apnoea is caused by the throat closing for short times during sleep. This closes the upper airway, so breathing stops. After a short time, the brain realises that breathing has stopped and triggers breathing again. This can sound like snoring.

Patient: So, you're saying that I stop breathing at night?

Nurse: That's right. In most cases, the person suffering from sleep apnoea doesn't even realise they are waking up and are surprised when they wake up exhausted.

Patient: I see. Now I understand why I have daytime sleepiness and I just can't concentrate on anything during the day.

Nurse: The important thing to remember about the condition is that it is not simply a form of insomnia or a type of snoring. If it is not managed properly, it can be a serious condition. People with severe sleep apnoea have an increased risk of car accidents and high blood pressure. They may also be more at risk of stroke and heart attack.

Patient: Oh, that sounds very serious.

Nurse: I can see it's a bit of a shock for you and a lot to take in, but there are somethings which will help you manage the condition.

Patient: Treatment, like medication?

Nurse: No, it doesn't involve medication. I'll explain a device you can use at night and also talk about some lifestyle changes which can be very effective.

Patient: Right. The doctor mentioned something about a special mask. Is that correct?

Nurse: That's right. It's called a CPAP mask. CPAP means continuous positive airways pressure. The mask looks a bit like an oxygen mask, but it works in a different way. It helps to increase pressure in your throat, so that your airways do not collapse and cause you to stop breathing.

Patient: How do I use it? I hope I don't have to wear it all day!

Nurse: You put the mask on in the same way as an ordinary oxygen mask. You only use it at night to make sure that you get a good night's sleep.

Patient: OK. That seems easy enough. What about the lifestyle changes you mentioned?

Nurse: Firstly, we advise you to avoid drinking alcohol or take medication which may make you sleepy.

Patient: I don't take any medication which makes me sleepy, but I do drink alcohol. Probably a bit too much, if I'm honest.

Nurse: How would you feel about not drinking alcohol or limiting your intake to a small amount?

Patient: I can try to cut down, but I can't see myself giving it up altogether.

Nurse: That's great that you are willing to consider cutting down. You might find it's easier to limit your alcohol intake gradually.

Patient: Is that the only lifestyle change I have to make?

Nurse: There is another thing which can make sleep apnoea worse. That's carrying excess weight. Have you noticed any change in your weight lately?

Patient: Yes, I started to pile on the weight, after the accident. I couldn't move about a lot for quite some time. But honestly, if I use this machine at night and get some sleep, I should be OK during the day. I might have a bit more energy.

Nurse: Yes, that's certainly true, however, excess weight, particularly in the neck area also plays a big part in your ability to breathe well, when you are lying down.

Patient: Well, I don't know…I've always had so much trouble losing weight. I think it would be too much for me to change, all at once.

Nurse: I appreciate that it seems overwhelming, but it really is very important to take as much pressure off your throat area. Remember that this is the area that is affected in sleep apnoea. The CPAP machine is very effective, but you can make it easier for the machine and yourself by losing even a small amount of weight.

Patient: You may be right, but I wouldn't know where to start with a diet.

Nurse: Would you be willing to look through this leaflet on nutrition and weight loss? As I said before, sleep apnoea can be a serious condition. It is very important that your condition is managed well to avoid complications.

Patient: OK, I'll read the leaflet and make an effort to lose weight. As you say, weighing even a little bit less has a positive effect.

Answers: Chapter 2: Scurvy

Cause	Symptoms	Treatment
deficiency Vitamin C	bleeding gums a bruise bruising	Vitamin C pill kiwi fruit mango

Chapter 3: Angry Relative

1. How does the nurse empathise and finds out why the patient's daughter is upset?

The nurse empathises (I can see that you're very upset.), then explains why she needs to understand more (she says it will help her understand what the problem is) and then asks an open question (Can you tell me a bit more about what's going on?)

2. What does the nurse NOT do, when the patient's daughter says 'You people are useless'?

The nurse tried not to take the comment personally and probably understands that the patient's daughter is just worried about her father.

3. How does the nurse confirm that she has understood what the problem is?

The nurse confirms that she has understood by summarising what she thinks the patient's daughter has said.

4. Instead of blaming the Recovery staff, how does the nurse manage the situation?

She empathises (I can understand that you might feel that way.) and then she gives an explanation of what is going to happen soon.

5. The nurse has to persuade the patient's daughter to leave her father in hospital, so he can have his operation. She does this in steps. What were they?

Step 1: Empathises (I know that it is hard when you have to wait so long) , then explains the importance of the operation (but it is very important that you have your operation.)

Step 2: The nurse acknowledges the patient's daughter's complaint (I agree that treatment schedules don't always go to plan) and repeats the importance of the operation (but it really is very important that your father stays in hospital). Finally, she asks for the patient's daughter's co-operation (Would you be willing to wait a bit longer before you make the decision to take your father home or not?)

Step 3: The nurse clarifies understanding (I understand what you are saying) and offers a solution (If I keep you up to date with what's happening, would you be willing to wait a bit longer?)

Poor Communication
1. Not explaining clearly
2. Interrupting Frequently
3. Assuming you understand without listening properly
4. Not clarifying information
5. Being reluctant to discuss sensitive or embarrassing issues
6. Using clichés
7. Being flippant
8. Having Poor Anger Management

9. Showing a Lack of Empathy
10 Not Giving Verbal   Feedback to show understanding
11 Not giving Non-Verbal Feedback to indicate interest

Chapter 4: IBS

1. Asking about the frequency of symptoms

How often have you had these symptoms?

2. Asking about the type of pain

Can you tell me what the pain's like?

3. Giving advice to a patient with IBS

But, you will need to cut out high fibre foods.

4. Confirming information

So, you have a type of colicky pain and flatulence. When you say that you have to keep going to the toilet, do you mean that you have diarrhea or constipation? Or both?

Questions

1. The nurse starts the conversation by ...

B   confirming that the patient has IBS

2. The nurse ...

A   clarifies the type of pain the patient experiences

3. The nurse clarifies information about...

B   the frequency of the episodes of diarrhoea

4. The nurse explains that stress...

C   may contribute to IBS

5. The nurse advises the patient to...

A   cut out high fibre foods

6. The IBS patient information leaflet contains...

B   contact details for the IBS Support Group

Chapter 4: Dog Bite

What does the nurse talk about with the patient?

1. treatment in hospital

2. care of the dressing at home

3. the importance of a tetanus injection

Explaining what is NOT going to be done.

1. Fortunately, the wound won't need any stitches.

2. These days it's more common not to stitch a dog bite.

3. It's better to leave the wound open to prevent infection.

Correct order of nurse's advice

do dressing every two days

nurse will give patient dressings to take home

don't get dressing wet, when showering

cover dressing with plastic bag, when showering

Persuading: Complete the dialogue

Nurse: No, unfortunately, dog bites are actually very dirty. And you need to protect yourself against tetanus.

Nurse: I can understand that you don't want an injection, if it's not necessary, but it really isn't advisable not to have a tetanus shot ,after a dog bite. It really is very important that you protect yourself against tetanus. It can be a serious disease.

Chapter 6: Sleep Apnoea

1. Sleep apnoea and its effect

2. CPAP

Language Functions in the Sleep Apnoea video
3. Explaining a health condition using everyday terms
Sleep apnoea is caused by the throat closing for short times during sleep. This closes the upper airway, so breathing stops. After a short time, the brain realises that breathing has stopped and triggers breathing again. This can sound like snoring.
1. Finding out the history of the problem:
Can you tell me what sort of health problems you've been having?
2. Signposting what you are going to talk about
I'll explain a bit about sleep apnoea and why it can be a serious problem, if you don't manage the condition.

Firstly, we advise you to avoid drinking alcohol or take medication which may make you sleepy.

5. Empathising
I can see it's a bit of a shock for you and a lot to take in,

I appreciate that it seems overwhelming

4. Reinforcing the importance of information
The important thing to remember about the condition is that it is not simply a form of insomnia or a type of snoring. If it is not managed properly, it can be serious condition.

I appreciate that it seems overwhelming, but it really is very important to take as much pressure off your throat area.

As I said before, sleep apnoea can be a serious condition.

6. Using non-judgmental language
How would you feel about not drinking alcohol or limiting your intake to a small amount?

8. Explaining medical terms

It's called a CPAP mask. CPAP means continuous positive airways pressure.

7. Encouraging a lifestyle change

How would you feel about not drinking alcohol or limiting your intake to a small amount?

Would you be willing to look through this leaflet on nutrition and weight loss?

9. Giving an alternative point of view

Yes, that's certainly true, however, excess weight, particularly in the neck area also plays a big part in your ability to breathe well, when you are lying down.

Kingsbury som dieapta